Secrets of Sport

The Technology that
Makes Champions

James de Winter

A & C Black • London

Produced for A & C Black by
Monkey Puzzle Media Ltd
48 York Avenue
Hove BN3 1PJ, UK

Published by A & C Black Publishers Limited
36 Soho Square, London W1D 3QY

Paperback published 2009
First published 2008
Copyright © 2008 A & C Black Publishers Limited

ISBN 978-1-4081-0017-2 (hardback)
ISBN 978-1-4081-0119-3 (paperback)

The right of James de Winter to be identified as the author of this Work has been asserted by him in accordance with the Copyright, Designs and Patents Act 1988.

A CIP catalogue record for this book is available from the British Library.

Editor: Cath Senker
Design: Mayer Media Ltd
Picture research: Laura Barwick
Series consultant: Jane Turner

This book is produced using paper that is made from wood grown in managed, sustainable forests. It is natural, renewable and recyclable. The logging and manufacturing processes conform to the environmental regulations of the country of origin.

Printed in China by C & C Offset Printing Co., Ltd

Picture acknowledgements
ActionPlus p. 14 (Tony Donaldson); CEDIP p. 10 (2007 CEDIP Infrared Systems); Corbis pp. 4 (Reuters), 17 (Reuters), 18 (Annebicque Bernard/ Sygma), 20 (Schlegelmilch); Equip2Golf p. 12 (Gary Mayes/golfballtest.org); Getty Images pp. 1 (WIN-Initiative), 5 (John Kelly), 6 left (Mark Nolan), 6 right (AFP), 7 (John Peters), 8 top (AFP), 11 (AFP), 13 (S Greenwood), 15 (Shaun Botterill), 16 (Bradley Ambrose), 19 (AFP), 22 (Jakubaszek), 23 (WIN-Initiative), 24 (VEER Elan Sun Star), 25 (Steve Satushek/Image Bank), 28 (Brian Bahr), 29; Hawk-Eye Innovations pp. 8 bottom, 9; PA Photos p. 27 (Kirsty Wigglesworth); Rex Features p. 21 (Sipa); Science Photo Library p. 26 (BSIP, CIOT).

The front cover shows athlete Oscar Pistorius competing in a 400-m race (Rex Features/ Olycom SPA).

CONTENTS

Abbreviations m stands for metres • **ft** stands for feet • **in** stands for inches •
km stands for kilometres • **km/h** stands for kilometres per hour • **mph** stands for miles per hour

Snowboard sandwich

We all know it's easy to slip over on ice and snow, but to move quickly in the right direction takes lots of practice. In the hands of a skilled rider, a snowboard is fast and easy to control.

Canadian snowboarder Jasey-Jay Anderson carves a turn. Slowing down transfers your energy to the snow and makes it spray up.

Wipeout

If you are moving very fast on a snowboard, it can be tricky to turn a corner. If you get it wrong, it's wipeout time!

The board is flexible. It bends as you turn.

wipeout   when a snowboarder falls over

You can change the shape of the edges of the board and sharpen them for better control.

There is a plastic layer on top of the **fibreglass** called a topsheet.
Top layer: plastic
Upper middle layer: fibreglass
Lower middle layer: wood
Bottom layer: plastic

The bottom layer is made of a super slippery plastic.

Adding wax to the bottom of this layer makes the board go

faster.

The middle is made of wood or foam to hold the shape, and coated in fibreglass for stiffness and strength.

A snowboard is made like a big sandwich by gluing layers of different materials together. Each layer has a special use.

fibreglass   material made from very thin, strong threads of glass

Slipper or football boot?

Modern football boots may look like slippers but they are carefully designed to allow the best possible control of the ball. This is useful when you're hoping to score with a curving free kick.

David Beckham is famous for his curving free kicks.

Stitched not laced

Early footballs were laced up, just like boots. Now they are made from 20 hexagons (six sides) and 12 pentagons (five sides), stitched tightly together to make an almost perfect sphere.

Curving the ball is useful in baseball too.

For a perfect curving free kick, you have to kick the ball so it spins as it moves forwards. The laces on the boot are sometimes covered by a flap to make it easier to kick a curve ball.

1 To make the ball curve, you need to make it spin.

2 The spinning changes the air flow around the ball.

3 This makes the ball curve as it moves.

4 The faster the ball is spinning, the more it curves.

Hawkeye: the ultimate tennis judge

In tennis matches, the ball moves so fast it can be hard to see what has happened. Arguments break out on the court. "That ball was in!" "No way, it was out!" A new system called Hawkeye could stop the arguments.

Serena Williams can hit a near perfect shot, but even her shots sometimes go out.

Hawkeye can prove where the ball bounced within a few millimetres. Here, the ball hit the line, so it was in.

Eyes of a hawk

Players use Hawkeye during training to help improve their game. It shows them where all their serves and shots landed.

IN

motion movement

The Hawkeye system uses multiple cameras around the tennis court. They record the **motion** of the ball – which travels as fast as a racing car. From the camera images, computers can estimate where the ball landed. The system is accurate to within a few millimetres.

The player served the ball from here.

A tennis serve can travel at over 200 km/h (125 mph), often too quick for human eyes to see where it bounces.

The ball is "out".

The ball landed on the wrong side of the court.

OUT

Snickometer: the cricket camera that sees sound

In cricket, the ball can travel at up to 160 kilometres per hour (100 miles per hour). It may only touch the bat for a few thousandths of a second. It's hard to see or hear exactly what has happened.

When you rub your hands together, you feel them getting hotter. The same thing happens when a fast cricket ball hits the bat. If the ball hits the bat, the spot where it hit will be hotter than the rest of the bat.

An **infra-red** camera makes it possible to see the 'hot spot' on the bat.

Where's cow corner?

The fielding positions in cricket have some odd names, including silly mid off, gully, short leg, fly slip and cow corner.

infra-red   energy that hot objects give off, which human eyes cannot see

The snickometer is a clever device that uses microphones to record the sound as the ball passes the bat. It checks if the ball has touched the bat.

If the ball touched the bat, you would see the peak on the **sound trace**.

If the ball passed the bat but didn't touch it, the snickometer would show there was no sound trace.

sound trace   the picture of a sound on a snickometer

Swing to win: the perfect golf game

Hit properly, a golf ball can travel nearly 500 metres (1,600 feet) in under six seconds!

Here you can see the inside and outside of a golf ball. The ball is made of a tough outer plastic skin with rubber or plastic inside.

It's not just about hitting the ball hard though. The design of the ball and the accuracy of the swing are vital to being a successful golfer.

What are the dimples for?

Most golf balls have between 300 and 500 dimples. The dimples help the air to move smoothly over the ball and make it go further.

driving hitting a long distance shot in golf

Although it is small, light and cheap to make, a modern golf ball is a high-tech piece of equipment.

Golf player Tiger Woods **driving**.

1 Kerpow!

The club touches the ball for less than one thousandth of a second.

2 The direction of the force must be almost perfect. Otherwise the ball will go in the wrong direction.

3 When the ball is hit, the **force** on it is more than the weight of a whole class of 30 students standing on it!

force a push or a pull on an object, making it move or change shape

Ice, high speeds and no brakes

Can you imagine sliding down a mountain on a tiny sled, feet first at almost 140 kilometres per hour (90 miles per hour)? On a luge, you have only a helmet and a skintight suit to protect you.

When you are riding a bike fast, you feel a force on your face and body slowing you down. This is called **air resistance**. If you lean forwards and bend your head down, the change in shape reduces the force. It becomes easier to ride. The same idea is used to design things to go as fast as possible.

Wheee!

You don't always need snow. Street luge is a popular sport.

air resistance the force of air pushing against a moving object

A luge rider in the Olympics.

A **STREAMLINED** shape makes it easy for air to flow over the rider, helping him to go as fast as possible.

The rider lies **flat** to reduce air resistance.

Runner

AIR

AIR

Runner

Skin-tight outfit further reduces air resistance.

No brakes!

The luge is one of the fastest winter Olympic sports. The luge has no brakes. To slow down, you push the runners of the sled together.

streamlined   with a smooth shape so it can move quickly through air or water

Sprint finishes – won by a nose?

*Horse racing is another sport that has split-second finishes. In athletics, you win if your **torso** crosses the line first. In horse racing, it's the horse whose nose passes first.*

Some sprinters run faster than you can ride your bike and finish the race at almost exactly the same time as each other. Could you decide who won in a split-second finish?

Loser!

torso   the main part of the human body from the neck to the top of the legs

*It's a **photo finish**. High-speed cameras photograph the end of the sprint race.*

Runners-up

In the 100 metres final at the 2004 Olympics, the first four runners finished within 4/100th of a second of each other.

The winner crosses the line.

Athletes lean forwards at the end of a race to push their torso over the line.

The red lines show who came first, second, third, and so on.

photo finish   when the end of a race is so close you need a photo to work out who won

Floating a boat

All boats need to float, but some also need to be strong, fast and almost impossible to capsize. In 2005 Ellen MacArthur braved gale-force winds and icebergs to complete a solo round-the-world trip in just 71 days.

The hull of a racing boat is made from tough materials. A strong, waterproof, outer skin keeps out the water. The honeycomb shape is for lightness and strength.

Make it waterproof

To build a boat, you need the right materials. The **hull** is made with super-strong, lightweight materials. Some useful materials, such as wood, are not waterproof. They are painted or coated in plastic.

capsize   when a boat turns upside down   **hull**   the main body or frame of a boat

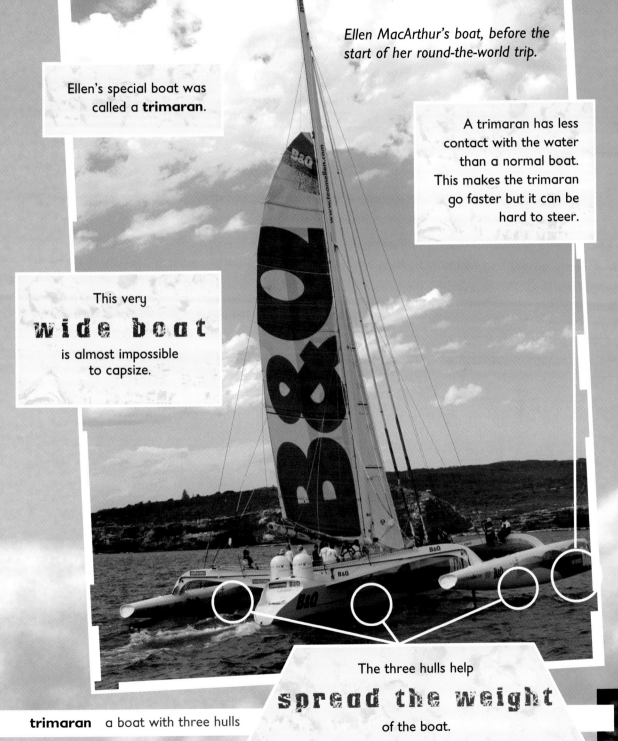

Ellen MacArthur's boat, before the start of her round-the-world trip.

Ellen's special boat was called a **trimaran**.

A trimaran has less contact with the water than a normal boat. This makes the trimaran go faster but it can be hard to steer.

This very **wide boat** is almost impossible to capsize.

The three hulls help **spread the weight** of the boat.

trimaran   a boat with three hulls

A £20,000 steering wheel!

Formula 1 racing is one of the most expensive sports in the world. Each car costs millions of pounds. Every single part is designed and tested by computer systems to make sure the car is a perfect machine.

A Formula 1 car racing at the Bahrain Grand Prix. This car can reach an incredible 320 km/h (200 mph).

Some racing cars can go from 0 to 160 kilometres per hour (100 miles per hour) in less than 8 seconds.

Pricey

You may only need one of them, but even the steering wheel for a Formula 1 racing car can cost more than £20,000.

The downwards force over the tail fin helps to hold the wheels to the ground and improve steering.

The flow of air over the car causes a downward force that helps it stay close to the ground.

The seat has fixed supports to hold the driver's head in place when turning sharp corners.

AIR

AIR

If the car is not steering well, the front fin can be moved during the race to increase or reduce the downwards force.

As air passes, it is guided into the engine to keep it cool.

The tyres can be changed during the race depending upon the weather conditions.

On your bike!

Whether you're racing or doing tricks, a BMX can be one of the most exciting ways to move around on wheels without an engine.

BMX bikes are strong and lightweight, with smaller wheels than racing bikes. This makes it easy to race, jump and move around when they are in the air.

Technical tricks like this take months to learn.

Errr...

Triple tail whip

This is one of the most difficult **BMX** tricks. The rider holds on to the handlebars and then spins the rest of the bike around three times.

grind   a BMX trick where you scrape the axle pegs against a hard surface

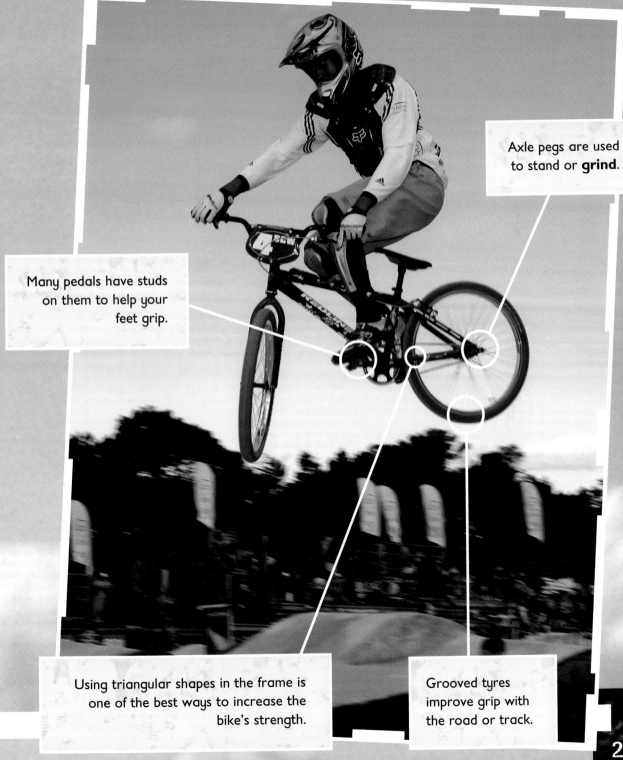

Axle pegs are used to stand or **grind**.

Many pedals have studs on them to help your feet grip.

Using triangular shapes in the frame is one of the best ways to increase the bike's strength.

Grooved tyres improve grip with the road or track.

23

It's a boo-wah day: hang gliding

A **boo-wah day** is a perfect day to jump off a cliff, attached to a hang glider. It's sunny, the sky is clear, and there's a gentle breeze. This is the closest you will ever come to flying like a bird.

Hang gliders can reach speeds over 75 km/h (47 mph) and heights of several kilometres.

As warm air rises above the cooler air below, it creates an upwards force, called lift, that is strong enough to keep the hang glider in the air.

If the lift force is greater than the **weight**, the glider will go up. If the upwards force is smaller than the weight, then the glider will go down.

boo-wah day a perfect day for hang gliding **weight** the force pulling objects to the ground

Gravity causes a downwards force called weight.

GRAVITY

Warm air provides a force lifting upwards.

LIFT

If the upwards force is the same as the weight then the glider will stay at a steady height.

Fly me to the Moon!

Well not quite. But in 2001, Austrian hang glider Manfred Ruhmer flew 700.6 kilometres (435 miles), taking the world distance record. It was further than the distance from London to Edinburgh.

gravity   the force that pulls objects towards the ground

Plug me in! Humans, computers and fitness

Bigger than you think

An adult's lungs can contain over 6 litres (10.5 pints) of air. That's enough to fill almost 20 empty drinks cans.

Athletes today aren't just found on the track. They often plug their bodies into a computer. Why do they do this?

During most kinds of exercise you need to increase your **heart rate**. Athletes use special equipment to measure their health and fitness. A portable heart rate monitor is small, light and easy to use. It measures how many times the heart beats every minute.

This man runs on a treadmill to test his fitness. He is wearing a face mask to measure how much oxygen he is taking in, and a monitor to measure his heart rate.

heart rate   the number of times the heart beats each minute

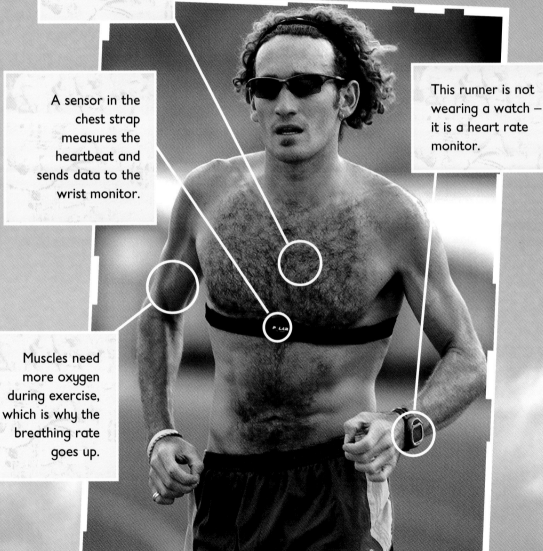

Athletes measure their **breathing rate** and heartbeat before and after they exercise. It helps them work out how successful their training has been and improve their training plan.

During exercise the heart and breathing rate will rise.

A sensor in the chest strap measures the heartbeat and sends data to the wrist monitor.

This runner is not wearing a watch — it is a heart rate monitor.

Muscles need more oxygen during exercise, which is why the breathing rate goes up.

breathing rate the number of breaths you take each minute

The blade runner: artificial legs

New strong and light materials have transformed sport for some athletes who previously couldn't compete in international competitions.

New, super-strong materials help athletes with a **physical disability** in many sports. Oscar Pistorius was born missing bones in the knee. He had his lower legs amputated (removed) when he was young. His artificial legs are made of a **composite** material that is designed to be strong and light. Oscar is known as "blade runner" because of the shape of his artificial legs.

These sportsmen play wheelchair basketball in special wheelchairs. They are strong, light and very easy to move around in.

physical disability   condition that means you cannot use a part of your body easily

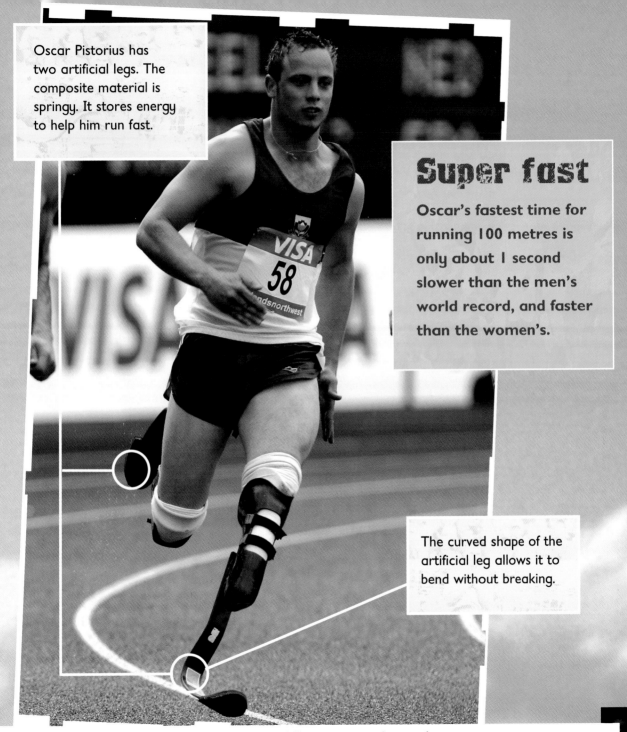

Oscar Pistorius has two artificial legs. The composite material is springy. It stores energy to help him run fast.

Super fast

Oscar's fastest time for running 100 metres is only about 1 second slower than the men's world record, and faster than the women's.

The curved shape of the artificial leg allows it to bend without breaking.

composite   a material made by joining different materials together

Glossary

air resistance the force of air pushing against a moving object

boo-wah day a perfect day for hang gliding

breathing rate the number of breaths you take each minute

capsize when a boat turns upside down

composite a material made by joining different materials together

driving hitting a long distance shot in golf

fibreglass material made from very thin, strong threads of glass

force a push or a pull on an object, making it move or change shape

gravity the force that pulls objects towards the ground

grind a BMX trick where you scrape the axle pegs against a hard surface

heart rate the number of times the heart beats each minute

hull the main body or frame of a boat

infra-red energy that hot objects give off, which human eyes cannot see

motion movement

photo finish when the end of a race is so close you need a photo to work out who won

physical disability condition that means you cannot use a part of your body easily

sound trace the picture of a sound on a snickometer

streamlined with a smooth shape so it can move quickly through air or water

torso the main part of the human body from the neck to the top of the legs

trimaran a boat with three hulls

weight the force pulling objects to the ground

wipeout when a snowboarder falls over